KT-871-431

It makes me ANGRY!

MARGARET COOLING

LION EDUCATIONAL

Oxford · Batavia · Sydney

Text copyright © 1990 Margaret Cooling

Published by
Lion Publishing plc
Sandy Lane West, Oxford, England
ISBN 0 7459 1577 9
Albatross Books Pty Ltd
PO Box 320, Sutherland, NSW 2232, Australia
ISBN 0 7324 0197 6

First edition 1990

Acknowledgments

Quotations and references
The following material is copyright and used by
permission:
Bible quotations are from the *Good News Bible*
copyright 1966, 1971 and 1976 American Bible
Society, published by the Bible Societies and
Collins
Page 18: Adrian Mitchell, 'Dumb Insolence', from
Strictly Private, Viking Kestrel
Page 20: account of the hunt protester, from
Wildlife Guardian, Issue 8, Summer 1988
Page 24: Roger McGough, 'Nooligan', from
In the Classroom, Jonathan Cape Ltd.

Design, graphics and illustrations
Simon Jenkins (except page 26)

Photographs
Barnaby's Picture Library/Ernest Robinson, page
17; Columbia Pictures Industries, Inc, page 30;
DAS Photography/David Simson, pages 10 (all),
24; Hodder & Stoughton, page 28; Mansell
Collection, page 26; Photo Co-op/Gina Glover,
page 13; Popperfoto, pages 6, 19, 25; Clifford
Shirley, cover; Zefa (UK) Ltd, page 14

British Library Cataloguing in Publication Data
Cooling, Margaret
It makes me angry.
1. Man. Anger. Control
I. Title
152.47

ISBN 0-7459-1577-9

Printed and bound in Yugoslavia

Contents

UNIT 1
What is anger? 4

UNIT 2
What causes anger? 6

UNIT 3
Anger in action 8

UNIT 4
**In case of emergency...
11**

UNIT 5
Anger in the home 14

UNIT 6
Anger in the classroom 17

UNIT 7
Violence and sport 19

UNIT 8
**Hooligans, vandals
and thugs 22**

UNIT 9
The angry brigade 25

UNIT 10
**Anger and forgiveness
28**

UNIT 11
**Gandhi and the
non-violent way 30**

Sometimes I want to explode!

How often have you felt like hitting someone when you are in a temper? Or kicking the dog? Do you ever slam the door when you are in a mood? Are you ever overcome with a desire to smash something really expensive when you are mad?

If you feel any of these things you are not alone. Anger is a very common emotion. It is not merely a personal matter. Anger is like a stone thrown into a pond – it sends out ever-widening waves. Uncontrolled anger makes waves in our personal lives, wrecking friendships and families.

At school, anger can lead to disruptive behaviour and even violence. Even our leisure can be ruined by the effects of aggression and violence. Many people fear going to football matches because of the behaviour of the fans. Uncontrolled anger in the local community can lead to vandalism and crime. On an international scale it can lead to war and terrorism.

This book explores all these different dimensions of anger – from our most private tantrums to the most public hijacks.

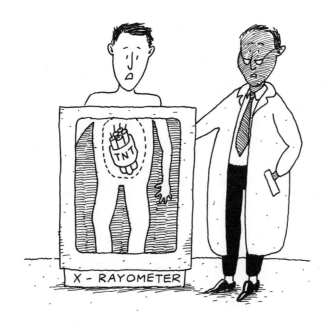

X - RAYOMETER

What is anger?

Anger affects people in different ways. Some people shout, slam doors and swing the cat around by its tail. Others go off and sulk in the corner. But however it affects us, we all send out warning signals to alert others to our anger. Here are just a few of the many warning signals...

He went redder and redder in the face and his eyes sort of BULGED!

He paced up and down the room

She ripped the telephone book in half – or at least she tried to!

She grabbed handfuls of her own hair and yanked them...

Her hands gripped the handlebars so tightly that her knuckles turned white

He banged his head again and again on the desk.

On red alert

Anger comes out in our actions and not just in our words. But what exactly goes on in our bodies when we get angry? When an aircraft carrier is threatened at sea, it goes into a state of 'red alert'. All the crew get to their battle stations, the aircraft scramble and the ship is made ready for battle. Here are some of the ways in which the human body goes into red alert when it is threatened...

■ The hypothalamus gland raises your body temperature
■ Your heart rate increases
■ Your breathing speeds up, bringing more oxygen into the lungs
■ Adrenalin is released, making you excited and quick to react
■ Your pupils dilate
■ Your digestion slows down and the amount of acid in your stomach rises
■ Your blood sugar level rises
■ Your blood pressure increases and the blood clots faster
■ Your muscles tighten

This whole chain of reactions is part of your body's defence mechanism. The body gears up to give you extra resources to fight an aggressor or to run for safety. Holding onto anger for a long time is not healthy because it keeps your body in the state of red alert. Staying angry can give you headaches, and if you have high blood pressure it can trigger a heart-attack.

Long-term anger is bad for you emotionally. It can wreck your friendships, leaving you lonely and isolated, and lead to bitterness or even hatred. Uncontrolled anger is a menace socially; it often leads to violence and aggression which have devastating results in the community.

Anger's relatives

Some people have strange relatives. Your great aunt Maud might be nothing like you but she is still a part of your family and therefore a relative of yours. Here are some of anger's relatives:

- bitterness
- resentment
- laughter
- extreme happiness
- fear
- excitement

Resentment and anger are obviously related to each other – but what about laughter? Although laughter and happiness may seem to be divorced from anger, your body reacts in the same way to these emotions too. When you next start laughing uncontrollably, check to see how your body is taking it all. You'll discover that your muscles are tight, your breathing is faster, your heart rate is up, etc.

This can also work in reverse. Just as we get a sense of elation when we are laughing, so we can feel this when we are angry. This is why some people enjoy being angry.

FOLLOW UP

1 Draw three overlapping circles. Label them: Anger, Laughter and Joy (as in the diagram). In each circle write what you feel like when you experience these emotions. Write sensations which are common to two or more of these experiences in the overlapping sections.

2 Find out more about the physical effects of anger from a nurse or doctor and design a poster with a government health warning on the effects of anger, medically, emotionally or socially.

3 Look back at the section on jealousy. Take one of the situations (for example Andy and Sita) and write a letter to an agony aunt from both partners, putting your point of view.

Jealousy (another member of the family)

Jealousy is also related to anger. We feel jealous when we are angry that others have something which we don't have. Jealousy can be expressed in many ways. It can be envy of wealth, position or relationships.

Look at these 'snapshots' of jealousy...

Karen is really angry with Kevin, her boyfriend. She was a few minutes late meeting him, and found him chatting to two other girls outside the chip shop. They were both very attractive, and Karen was jealous.

Charlotte was jealous of her younger sister, Suzie. Their parents always gave Suzie much more expensive birthday presents than the ones they bought for Charlotte.

Andy was furious with Sita. They had just had a blazing row at the disco, and she had deliberately danced during a slow number with one of his mates.

Jealousy can be extremely destructive. Some people treat others almost as if they were their personal possessions. But very occasionally jealousy can be positive. It can act as a warning signal, telling us to protect a precious relationship. Jealousy is wrong when we use it selfishly to possess people and objects.

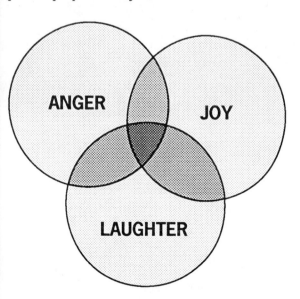

What causes anger?

Lenny was playing darts at the youth club. Earlier that day he had failed an important exam at school and his father had given him a hard time about it when he had got home. Lenny had raided his parents' drinks cupboard and arrived at the youth club only half sober.

Then Paul, one of his mates, made the mistake of laughing when one of Lenny's darts thudded uselessly into the wall. Lenny turned on Paul and started laying into him. The two of them had to be pulled apart.

What caused Lenny's anger? Paul's laughter?

Police in riot gear, carrying protective shields, find a burning car in Brixton, 1985. Riots broke out after the police accidentally shot a black woman.

The two cans of lager? His father's telling-off? Or failing the exam?

Anger and violence are facts of life which have dogged mankind since the beginning of time. There's nothing new about anger and violence. The human race has merely worked out bigger and nastier ways of being violent and labelled it progress. Roman armies killed a million with the sword. We can do it quicker!

What are the causes of anger and violence within us? Are we naturally violent or is it something we learn? There are many different theories about the causes of anger and violence, some of which are described briefly here.

Outside causes

Outside factors such as alcohol and drugs are often blamed for violence. Drink and drugs can encourage aggressive behaviour by 'turning off' parts of the brain that normally keep our aggression under control. Other people argue that alcohol and drugs don't actually cause violence. They simply release the anger which is already there inside us.

Overcrowding, bad housing and the media are all blamed for violence, but none of these are automatic causes. Belgium and Holland are both densely populated, but neither are known as violent countries. Not everyone who watches violent TV programmes reacts violently.

There are other possible outside causes. Many blame anger and violence on society. They believe we are not naturally violent, it is something we learn from those around us. There may be a lot in this. Children brought up in violent homes often grow up to be violent themselves.

Inside causes

There's another side to the argument. Some people say that anger and aggression aren't things that we learn – we are already like this deep inside ourselves. They say we are naturally violent and the pent-up aggression we feel needs an outlet. Violence is like a volcano blowing its plug, or a dam opening its gates. It is merely a natural way of releasing pent-up emotions.

The idea underneath this view is that human beings are animals, and like other animals we are aggressive. This is OK, but what is dangerous is lack of control. However, humans are far more aggressive than most animals. We are the only animals to go in for mass murder and torture. Animals seem to control themselves much better than we do.

For some people, frustration is the main cause of their anger. Life is a bit frustrating for everybody. But for those who feel powerless, with no job, little education, and few hopes, the anger and frustration can spill over into violence.

A more optimistic view sees humanity as capable of perfecting itself. People who believe this say that we have the ability to rise above our animal nature. We are able to use love to deal with our aggression.

Others find hope in human history, because history is about change. Society may be violent now, but we can change it. This theory puts the responsibility firmly on our shoulders. We hold the solution to our problems in our own hands. We cannot blame anyone else.

These are very different theories about humanity. Human beings are violent animals or potential saints. We are either totally controlled by our animal nature or totally responsible for what we do.

The religious dimension

Religions such as Christianity, Judaism and Islam do not see humans as animals or saints. Instead, they see us as good but faulty. Humanity is like a dress bearing the label of a brilliant designer, but with a fault in the fabric. The design is still good but it is not what the designer intended. It is like driving a sports car with a steering fault. The car might be great but it keeps veering to one side.

Religious people call this fault 'sin' or 'evil'. Christians, for example, are neither pessimists nor optimists. Looking at a violent society they would say the fault and the responsibility lies with humanity. But people cannot put themselves or the world right without God's help.

FOLLOW UP

Squashing a spider
Attacking a member of a racial minority

1 Here is a top ten of violence. Score each violent act on a scale of one to ten (1–3 = not very violent, 4–6 = quite violent, 7–10 = very violent).

Hitting a friend
Using an atomic weapon
Mugging
Rape
Verbal abuse
A rider whipping a horse
A football fan kicking a rival fan
A parent smacking a child

2 Think of a time recently when you became really angry. Try filling in the spaces below.
I became angry because .... (what were the real reasons for getting angry?)
I lost my temper because .... (what sparked off your anger?)
I was angry with .... (your parents? your friends? the dog?)
I was glad I was angry because .... (did any good come out of it?)
I was sorry I was angry because .... (did any bad come out of it?)

Anger in action

You are invited to
A FIGHT
between
Jeff (2-ton) Davis
and
'Killer' Reynolds

behind the
Bike Sheds
3.45 pm

As we saw earlier, anger expresses itself in many different ways. Some people inwardly seethe, while others outwardly explode, causing damage and destruction. It's easy to spot anger when someone throws a book at you, but how do you spot the less obvious forms of anger?

Spot the angry person

There are lots of ways of letting someone know you are angry. Try writing a quick story or a short sketch about some of the following...

■ **Angry actions** People have a whole range of actions to use then they are angry. Thumping someone. Talking behind his or her back. Stopping a game by walking off with the football. Slamming the door. Pushing a cream trifle into someone's face.

■ **Angry signals** Sometimes we can make people aware that we are angry without saying a word. There's the look that could kill. Turning your back on someone. Shaking your fist. Making a V-sign. Or simply staring someone down.

■ **Angry words** Think of the type of things people say when they are angry.

There are insults. People call each other names; or compare them with unpleasant substances or objects. Or they say things that are calculated to be especially hurtful to the other person. Old wounds are painfully opened up. Why do you think people often swear when they are cross?

■ **Angry tones** It is not just the words you say that matter, it is the way that you say them. Even pleasant words can be said with a snarl. Phrases like 'Thank you very much', 'I really love you' and 'I hope you're happy' can mean the opposite when they are said with enough venom.

Communication is a complex business. When you are trying to work out whether someone is angry or not, remember to look at the way they use their body and their tone of voice as well as listening to their words.

Three types of anger

Anger comes in roughly three forms: rage, resentment, and a creative type of anger, sometimes called indignation.

■ **Rage** is destructive anger. Your temper goes out of control. The result is often verbal abuse or physical violence.

■ **Resentment** is anger that has gone underground. Resentment quietly seethes under the surface. It is less obvious than rage, but it can be more deadly.

■ **Indignation** is anger used for good. It tries to correct a situation that has gone wrong. It does not simply hit out at the wrongdoer. This type of anger can be used on behalf of yourself or other people.

Rage and resentment are destructive, but indignation is creative. Indignation refuses to allow people to be treated in an unacceptable way. In some situations, anger can show that we care enough to act.

Women and anger

A striking example of indignation took place at the beginning of this century. The suffragettes were women who believed that all women should have the right to vote in political elections. Until 1918, only men could do this.

The suffragettes began their campaign by trying to persuade politicians of their view. But they were ignored. Their anger at this led to a number of confrontations with the authorities...

■ Women chained themselves to the railings outside 10 Downing Street
■ 120 suffragettes smashed thousands of pounds' worth of shop windows in London's West End
■ They bombed a prominent politician's house – no one was hurt
■ One suffragette threw herself under the King's horse at the Derby and was killed
■ Other suffragettes went on hunger strike in prison and were force-fed

All of these actions can be said to be acts of anger against a wrong situation.

God gets angry

In the Old Testament, which is considered holy by both Jews and Christians, even God gets angry at those who cause other people suffering. His anger is not rage or resentment, but indignation on behalf of the poor who are cruelly treated by the rich. One of the Old Testament prophets, Amos, thunders out God's words...

'Listen to this, you that trample on the needy and try to destroy the poor of the country. You say to yourselves, "We can hardly wait for the holy days to be over so that we can sell our corn. When will the Sabbath end, so that we can start selling again? Then we can overcharge, use false measures, and tamper with the scales to cheat our customers. We can sell worthless wheat at a high price. We'll find a poor man who can't pay his debts, not even the price of a pair of sandals, and we'll buy him as a slave."

'The Lord, the God of Israel, has sworn, "I will never forget their evil deeds. I will turn your festivals into funerals and change your glad songs into cries of grief." '

Amos 8:4–7,10

Creative anger in action

William Booth, the founder of the Salvation Army, worked among the poor in nineteenth-century London. He was angry at the terrible poverty he witnessed in the East End. He saw children starving and ill-clothed and parents out of work, their lives wrecked by drink. He saw the dreadful conditions they lived in, often the whole family lived in one filthy, rat-infested room.

William Booth spent his life working to change those conditions and telling people of the love of God. His anger fuelled his campaign.

FOLLOW UP

1 Make a list of unacceptable behaviour and situations about which it is right to feel angry...
• At school
• At home
• Among your friends

2 Look at the three situations below. Each one ends at the point where one of the characters might get angry. Working in groups of three or four, choose one story. Take a few minutes to write down how you see the story ending. Now read out your endings and discuss as a group which you think is the fairest to all the story's characters.

• Carol had promised her mum that she wouldn't skip school any more. The school had already warned her that she would be suspended if it happened again. Then one day, while she was out shopping, Carol's mum saw Carol with a friend from school. Her mum...

• Jeff was furious when his French teacher yelled at him for forgetting his book. He was sure he had given it in.

The next day his French teacher said the book had turned up, he had left it in the staff room by mistake. He didn't even apologise! Jeff seethed and...

• Cathy had only been in the school two weeks and everyone took the mickey out of her because of her accent. She dreaded English, they all had to speak for two minutes on a given subject and it was her turn today. When she began to speak they were strangely quiet. For a moment she thought it was going to be OK. Then she realized that they were doing their best to stare her out. She began to redden, then she lost her place, she felt angry inside and...

3 Think of some times when you have felt...

• Rage (when you've been angry and lost control of your actions)
• Resentment (when you seethed inside but didn't show it)
• Indignation (when you were angry for someone else)

How did each of these types of anger make you feel at the time? How do you feel about them now?

In case of emergency...

Anger can be a lethal weapon. The things we do or say in anger can wound others and leave permanent scars on our relationships. Here are just a few examples...

After what she said that time, I'll never believe again that she loves me...

GEOFF, 17

A DIVORCED MOTHER

I didn't mind him hitting me so much. It was when he started hitting the kids in the same way that I knew our marriage was dead.

I don't let anyone talk to me like that. I sacked him on the spot as soon as he said it!

THE MANAGING DIRECTOR

He just told me to get out of the car. It took me two hours to get home, in the rain, in the dark. I'll never speak to him again!

NICKY, 22

Like pain, anger is part of the body's warning system. Anger tells us to beware. It equips us to fight but it says...

Look out! You're in a dangerous state!

Because anger can be so deadly, we have to be extra careful with it. So what can we do about our anger?

First-aid
When there is an accident, first-aid is often applied. For example, you might immobilise a broken leg to prevent damage. First-aid is only a temporary treatment. It buys you time, but it is not a permanent cure.

Anger often needs a sort of first-aid treatment. Sometimes you can feel so angry that you have to buy time so that you can decide how to react and regain control over your behaviour.

This unit looks at some short-term measures aimed at slowing you down when you are angry. They allow you a bit of time to think. First-aid should never take the place of treatment. And in the same way, you should always sort out the real problem that caused you to be angry in the first place.

The cure
The bad news is that there is no permanent cure for anger. There is

11

First-aid measures

The next time you feel really angry try some of the following...

• Remove yourself from the thing/person/situation that is making you angry.
• Tell yourself you are not going to explode.
• Ask yourself if the situation is worth getting angry about.
• Divert your attention, busy yourself with something else that will take your mind off your anger.
• Do something you enjoy to relax yourself: listen to a record, watch television, have a long, hot bath.
• Channel the energy anger creates in another way: run, swim, go for a walk, or thump a pillow.
• Talk with friends, talk to yourself, or write down why you are angry.
• Laugh if the situation deserves it, cry if it doesn't.

Remember: Don't make important decisions or judgments about people while you are angry. Things may look very different when you calm down.

nothing we can do to guarantee that we will never get angry again. But the good news is that we can learn to control how we express our anger to other people.

The following stories show how some people learned to control their anger.

Vicky had waited for an hour in the rain before Mark showed up. He said sorry and mentioned something about trouble at work. She was just about to give him a mouthful when she remembered she had done the same to him last week. Now she knew what it felt like.

Mick's Dad lent him the car to take his girlfriend out. He wanted to impress her with his driving skills but he kept stalling it. At first he became embarrassed, then angry. What should have been a great night was turning out all wrong. At that point he decided he was not going to ruin the evening. Instead he laughed, and he and Lynn laid bets on whether he would stall the car the next time he slowed down.

Sharon was usually in a bad mood by ten o'clock. Today was different. She had just got a job. That morning her younger brother's teasing failed to rile her. She missed the bus and didn't care. Even her friend Teresa's sarcasm only raised a smile. Every time she felt angry she just thought about her new job instead.

Gary was quick-tempered and he knew it, but he also knew he could not afford to get into trouble any more. Counting to ten had been no use; he was still hopping mad when he got to fifty. Kicking a football seemed to work, though. Whenever Gary was really mad he kicked the football against the wall as hard as he could. His temper gradually improved – so did his football.

Matt looked at the computer in despair. His friend Paul had accidentally wiped his disc clean and it had taken him ages to type his homework in. He felt angry, but what could he do? If he hit out at Paul he could lose a friend as well as his homework. He needed to hand the work in in the morning. Matt walked out of the room to calm down. Then he forced a grin and said, 'I hope you can type.'

Zara watched as a group of fourth-years stopped young children on their way home from Primary School. They demanded money from them and frightened them. Zara was really angry. Her anger made her overcome her fear. She felt she had stood by long enough. Now she wanted to do something about it. She talked it over with her parents and informed the head of the Primary School without giving any names. The head stationed a teacher at the gates, which deterred the fourth years.

Martin had always done well at school and tended to let others know it. The crunch came when he had to do CDT for the first time. He was hopeless. He felt angry and humiliated when others laughed at his efforts. He had seldom experienced real anger, but now he understood how other people felt when they failed. From that moment on he tried to put himself in other people's shoes and imagine how they felt, rather than boasting about what he could do.

There may be no permanent cure for anger but there is treatment. Christians believe that one of the main causes of anger is the bias to wrongdoing within each one of us. Anger can also result from insecurity. People do not think they are loved or lovable, and they take out their feelings of insecurity on others in the form of anger.

The message of Christianity is twofold. First, Christians believe that in Jesus God has dealt with the problem of sin. Anyone who comes to him can receive help to deal with present wrong. Secondly, the Christian message is about a God who loves even the unlovable.

FOLLOW UP

1 Try to keep an Anger Diary. Try keeping the diary for five school days. Each time you are angry, write down in a notebook the answers to these questions...

- Who made you angry?
- What did they do or say to make you angry?
- How were you angry?

At the end of the week, look at your diary. What makes you most angry – people, situations, things that go wrong, or yourself? Do you tend to explode and throw things around, or do you just quietly seethe inside?

2 Which of the first-aid suggestions are you most likely to use? Can you add any other ways of coping with anger to this list?

3 Design a board game on anger. You will need a pile of red cards on which you write penalties for angry situations. Examples: 'Go back two places for hitting your younger brother for borrowing your Walkman without asking.'
You will also need a pile of green cards which reward situations where people deal with anger positively. Example: 'Go forward one square. You sat through a TV programme you hated because your sister wanted to watch it.' Think up the situations for the cards. Then design the board with red and green squares, so that when you land on either colour you pick up a card.

It's easy to be angry with people when they aren't there to defend themselves. One of the best ways to deal with anger is to talk to the person you're angry with, or to talk with friends who know you both.

Anger in the home

Why do husbands batter wives? And why do wives put up with it? This unit looks at this disturbing subject.

Anger and violence often erupt in the home. Here are five frightening facts about violence at home...

■ In June 1988, baby Dean Scott was left to starve to death, although his parents made sure they fed the dog.

■ In one area of Liverpool in 1874, 160 wives died because their husbands beat them.

■ Every year, between 150 and 200 children in Britain die because their parents abuse or neglect them.

■ 25 per cent of all assaults reported to the police are assaults on wives. Even so, most cases of wife-battering are not reported.

■ In the year 1987–88, the NSPCC responded to more than 21,000 reports of alleged cruelty, involving over 42,000 children.

Wife-battering

In this unit, we will be looking at the main form of violence in the home – wife-battering. We will then be looking at the friction between parents and young people.

Why do women put up with violence from their husbands? Many do because they still love their husbands. Others fear leaving home because of financial insecurity, or they may fear their children going into care.

WHAT'S WRONG WITH...?

Teenagers

- Teenagers are rude and show no respect
- They don't know the meaning of hard work
- Teenagers want to be treated as adults – but without the responsibility
- They treat parents like cheque books with legs!
- Some of them seem to delight in intimidating people
- Teenage dress, music and general behaviour is dreadful

Do you agree with any of these?

Parents

- Parents want us to be like them
- They are always afraid of what others will think
- Parents are boring
- Parents are bossy and think they have all the answers
- They are easily offended
- They're jealous because they didn't enjoy themselves much when they were young

Which of these statements do you think are true?

Battered women can now seek help in one of the many women's refuges opening up around the country. In 1973 the first Women's Refuge was set up in Brixton, and in one year (1977) in the Chiswick Refuge alone, 1,122 mothers and children were taken in.

What causes wife-battering?
There is no single cause of wife-battering, though there are many possible ones. Which of the following would you say contributed substantially to wife-battering? Discuss these in groups and give them a score out of ten, depending on how important you think they are (10 = very important, 1 = not at all important).

- Men are naturally aggressive. It's just that some men are a bit more aggressive than others.
- It's a matter of sexual frustration which sometimes leads to violence.
- It's the result of a disturbed mind.
- It's part of the destructive side of mankind that we all have in different ways.
- Violence is learned from people around us. Violent men come from violent families.
- Violence is the result of male dominance which encourages men to treat women as objects.

■ Violence is the result of outside factors such as unemployment, alcohol abuse, money worries, poor housing, drugs or ill health.

If these are a few of the reasons why some men batter their wives, what prevents other men from doing the same? What is it about many marriages that makes them non-violent? Which of the following factors do you think are important in reducing violence? Score them 1–10, where 1 = not at all important, and 10 = very important.

- The couple control their tempers better.
- The men do not see women as inferior. You do not batter someone you believe is your equal.

Unit 5

The 10 things I like most about parents.

■ They can talk to each other about their differences.

■ They have other ways of coping with anger besides violence.

■ Their living conditions are good.

■ They don't use drugs or excessive alcohol.

■ They have a lot of support from others.

■ The women have a positive view of themselves. They stand up to the men if there is aggression.

■ Both partners are mentally stable. They probably come from homes where there was little or no violence.

The generation gap

Most homes are not violent but there is often anger between adults and their teenage children. Many parents think their children come from another planet and the friction between teenage children and their parents often causes anger and conflict. Look at these two stories. Who do you think is at fault in each of them?

Clare had promised her parents that she would look after the house while they were away. She hadn't washed up since they left and her friends had been around until late last night.

She looked at the house. Someone had burnt a hole in the settee with a cigarette. The carpet was a mess. There was half-eaten food everywhere. The neighbours had complained about the noise last night, and she knew they would say something to her mum. Her mum didn't like her friends. She said they were rude, they dressed appallingly and played terrible music.

She said they frightened the neighbours.

Clare could hear now the lecture she would get about always asking for money and never doing anything in return. Always wanting to be treated like an adult and never taking responsibility. Etc, etc, etc.

Nick's mum was fed up. It was Monday, it was her lunch-hour, and Nick was still in bed. Nick could see no point in getting up. He had lost his place on the YTS scheme and couldn't find a job. There was nothing to get up for. His mum said he didn't look hard enough for work. She felt ashamed of him in front of the neighbours. He looked a sight and slouched about doing nothing.

His mum thought he ought to help around the house as she was out at work all day. He thought she was boring and bossy and probably jealous because she never had much fun. If she tried to say anything to him he just bristled. They didn't seem to be able to talk to each other without having a row.

FOLLOW UP

1 Find out about the help available for battered women from:
The Women's Aid Federation
PO Box 391
Bristol BS99 7WF

2 Try to find out about Women's Refuges. If there is a local refuge in your area, try to conduct an interview with one of the workers.

3 Conduct a class survey on the Top Ten Things You Like About Parents. If it's possible, you could also conduct a survey among parents on their top ten for teenagers.

4 Look at the 'What's Wrong With...?' box. Choose any one item and say how conflict over that issue could be reduced in the home.

Anger in the classroom

Schools are not all angry and violent places but violence does exist in some schools and some say it is increasing. Within a school there can be protection rackets, attacks on teachers, vandalism and bullying. What causes some schools to be angry and violent places and others to be more peaceful?

One reason is powerlessness and the way those in power use their authority. A lot of anger is caused by feeling other people are in control of your life. This sometimes results in anger against all those who do have power: teachers, parents, the police and adult society in general. Sometimes violence is learnt in the home and is imported into school. Sometimes a school can reflect the violent community it serves.

Types of anger

Anger can come in many forms. At one end of the spectrum, anger expresses itself in acts of physical violence, but most people express their anger in other ways. Below are some of the activities which pupils get suspended for. Which of these do you think is the most serious?

- Insolence to teachers and verbal abuse
- General bad behaviour
- Refusal to accept school discipline
- Bullying
- Playing truant
- Not keeping school rules
- Disrupting lessons
- Behaving violently towards teachers
- Being a bad influence on others
- Stealing and damaging school property

Some people do not express their anger openly but they make it felt all the same. Look at the poem, *Dumb Insolence*, in the box on the next page.

The boy in this poem is angry with everyone. How does he get at other people without getting into trouble? How do you think people react to this type of behaviour?

What causes classroom violence?
A number of suggestions have been made about what causes violence and aggression at school. Which of the following do you think are right?

- **Not enough control in the early years** Some children come to school at five already totally resistant to authority. Daren was like this. His parents had brought him up to do whatever he liked, and when he had been badly behaved, they had either ignored him or had been amused at his antics. He made life at his nursery school a misery from day one.

Some school fights (like this one) aren't serious. But the ugly side of school violence includes bullying, threats, blackmail and protection rackets.

DUMB INSOLENCE

I'm big for ten years old
Maybe that's why they get at me
Teachers, parents, cops
Always getting at me
When they get at me
I don't hit em
They can do you for that
I don't swear at em
They can do you for that
I stick my hands in my pockets
And stare at them
And while I stare at them
I think about sick
They call it dumb insolence
They don't like it
But they can't do you for it
I've been done before
They say if I get done again
They'll put me in a home
So I do dumb insolence

Adrian Mitchell

■ **Lack of attention** Some children receive very little attention at school and at home. Nicola's parents were always working, when they weren't flopped in front of the TV. Nicky had lots of toys and her own telly, but her mum and dad never noticed her. The only way to get attention at home was to do something bad. Nicola carried this behaviour over into the classroom.

■ **Conflicting values** In some homes the values the parents live by are not the values of the school and the child is caught in a conflict. James' parents were always telling him to hit back and stick up for himself. The teacher on the other hand was always trying to stop fights and teach the children other ways of solving problems.

■ **Problems at school** Schools are often understaffed and teachers are not adequately trained to deal with aggressive situations. This came home to David Jones when he started teaching. He felt totally unprepared. His teaching took up all his time, but what really exhausted him was the constant aggro. Often he was too tired, too busy, or lacked the skill to sort out the problems that faced him.

■ **Television** Many are concerned about the television programmes pupils watch and the influence they have. This came home to one Primary School when they did a survey as part of media studies. They were shocked by the amount of TV watched, and worried by the late-night viewing of totally unsuitable programmes.

FOLLOW UP

1 Look at the poem. What types of behaviour do people indulge in which don't get them into trouble, but are planned to annoy and anger? If you were a teacher, what would make you most angry: dumb insolence, or more obvious disruptive behaviour?

2 Look at the list of activities pupils get suspended for. What do you think the effect is...
• on the person doing it
• on the teacher
• on the rest of the class
• on the school as a whole

3 Make a list of the most common forms of anger and violence in your school. How do you think your school could best deal with them?

Violence and sport

Sport is sometimes proposed as a peaceful way of getting rid of aggression. People argue that it is better to be aggressive on the football field than on the streets. However, sport has many problems with violence, both on the field and among the fans. The sports themselves are not all peaceful. Three hundred boxers world-wide have been killed since 1945, and at least ten boxers have died after fights in British rings in the last forty years. Even sports such as football, cricket and rugby can cause injury – and, very occasionally, death.

Football violence

In 1909, more than 6,000 spectators went on the rampage at Hampden Park in Glasgow. The goal posts were torn up, pay booths were burnt and many houses around the ground were destroyed. Football violence is not new, but it is on the increase.

In May 1985, forty-two people were killed and 400 injured in the tragedy at Belgium's Heysel stadium. Shocked TV viewers watched as rioting Liverpool fans charged Z block, causing death and injury in the panic.

A shocked Italian fan carries his injured friend to safety after the Heysel Stadium disaster in May, 1985.

Hunt protester attacked

The Kennelman of the New Forest Foxhounds has been fined £300 plus £150 compensation for an attack on anti-hunt protester Mr Gary Colbourne. Colin Haley pleaded guilty to Actual Bodily Harm against Mr Colbourne.

The court heard that Mr Colbourne was sitting in his car in a car park when Haley suddenly reached in through the open window, grabbed him and punched him in the face. Mr Colbourne attempted to protect himself by winding up the window, so Haley ripped off the CB aerial and attempted to hit Mr Colbourne with it through the partially closed window.

Haley said his actions had been a result of 'provocation' by anti-hunt protesters which he claimed had occurred throughout the season and, while Mr Colbourne was not to blame for the provocation, Haley looked upon him as one of the same group.

Haley has now left the New Forest Foxhunt for a new hunting job in Lincolnshire.

Most of the people killed were Italian fans. As a result, England was banned from entering European football matches, a decision which was confirmed when English fans went on the rampage in Dusseldorf in June 1988.

The British government have called upon the football clubs to take tough measures. But what can really be done? Here are some of the suggestions that have been made...

1. Segregate rival groups of fans.
2. Better policing and more police at matches.
3. Regulate ticket sales.
4. Stiffer penalties for offenders.
5. Take away passports of known offenders.
6. Stop the sale of alcohol near the grounds.
7. Identity cards.

There are no easy solutions to this problem, as the tragic events at Hillsborough in 1989 demonstrated. Many people were crushed as fans poured onto the terraces. The very barriers that help solve the problem of pitch invasion contributed to the tragedy. Any solutions to the problem of violence need to take account of public safety.

Football is not the only sport where fans get violent. Violence has also flared at cricket matches in both the West Indies and Pakistan. In 1988, small groups of fans caused trouble at a few cricket matches in England. Is the violence really attached to the particular sport, or does the sport provide an occasion when people feel they can let their anger loose?

Some people say that sports like football, rugby and cricket are bound to attract violence because they are competitive. One person or team wins only when it has beaten the other side. Sports like these are said to encourage violence because they pit people against each other.

The fans of different football clubs become like tribes that go to war against each other on Saturday afternoons. The seriousness of this warfare is shown by the heavy police presence at most games, the high mesh fences used to cage fans in, and the way in which rival groups are strictly segregated. The police regularly confiscate an assortment of horrific home-made weapons from fans attempting to smuggle them into the stands. Sharpened screwdrivers, heavy bolts, concealed hammers and nails top the list.

However, it is not easy to make a solid connection between competition in sport and violence among the fans. A majority of football, rugby and cricket supporters are not violent. And what about boxing fans? You never see headlines about crowd trouble at what must be one of the most openly violent sports.

Blood sports

Blood sports involve the hunting and killing of animals. In medieval Britain, there was a whole range of blood sports: bear-baiting, cock-fighting, arranged dog-fights and many different types of hunting and shooting. Some of these have survived. In modern Spain, bull-fighting is enormously popular. In Britain, fox-hunting, deer-hunting and hare-coursing are still legally allowed.

These sports provoke demonstrators to anger and violence.

People who feel strongly about blood sports sometimes try to disrupt them. Do you think their anger is justified? Are there limits to what people should do to disrupt hunting?

Boxing: blood sport?

On 4 November 1980, one man died after being repeatedly punched in the head by another man. The police brought no charges, because the punches were delivered during a boxing match. Johnny Owen, a 24-year-old bantamweight never recovered after losing consciousness during the fight for the world title in Los Angeles. He died six weeks later.

These quotes from famous boxers give an inside view of the sport:

You can knock a man down with a blow to the jaw, but he'll get up fighting. Hit him hard enough and often enough in the mid-section, and he'll go down for keeps.

Jack Dempsey

Every punch was thrown with bad intentions. I was there to fight, not to play.

Mike Tyson

Tyson hit me on top of my head in the first round and it felt like my neck went down to my belly button.

Mike Jameson

FOLLOW UP

1 Why do you think there is crowd violence at football matches, but not at boxing matches?

2 Look at the section on boxing. Do you think this sport should be banned? Give your reasons, for or against.

3 Try to devise a game (it could be outdoor or indoor) in which there is no competition at all. Base your game on co-operation and teamwork. To give you some ideas, mountain-climbing is one sport that relies on co-operation.

4 Run a survey of people in your school to find out opinions on blood sports. Draw your results on a bar graph. You can send for information on blood sports from: The League Against Cruel Sports, Sparling House, 83-87 Union Street, London SE1 1SG.

Hooligans, vandals and thugs

Uncontrolled anger can have devastating effects in the local community. It can lead to crimes such as mugging and vandalism which present serious problems, particularly in the inner city.

In 1987, the police recorded 141,042 cases of violence against the person in England and Wales.
589,000 cases of criminal damage were reported in the same year. There were also 32,633 cases of robbery.

The cost of vandalism to local authorities is astronomical. But the cost in terms of people's lives and the environment can never be counted.

Mugging

Anger can spill over into violence, but who are its victims? How much do you know about this?

There seems to be a contradiction here. Men are most likely to be victims, but women are the most afraid. Are women cowards, sheltering behind locked doors for no good reason, or are there ways of explaining this contradiction?

The reasons why more men appear to be attacked may be because women, on the basis of previous experience, take steps to avoid attack. Some women may be hesitant to report crime for various reasons, so those attacks do not show up in the statistics. Men may also be reluctant to admit to fear because of their 'macho image'. Women and the elderly are not irrationally afraid of violence. They

Who are most likely to be the victims of violence: men, women, or the elderly?

According to the figures, men are the most likely victims.

Who is the most afraid of assault, and whose lives are most affected by it?

Women and the elderly — a large proportion of whom are women.

Vandals, thugs and hooligans

Did you know?

The Vandals were a fierce German tribe who lived during the time of the Roman Empire. They swept over much of Europe and North Africa, wreaking havoc and leaving a trail of destruction in their wake.

The Thugs were an Indian religious sect who murdered their enemies by strangling or poisoning. They are the basis for the film *Indiana Jones and the Temple of Doom*.

The Hooligans were probably an Irish family in the last century whose unruly behaviour put the word in the dictionary.

are its hidden victims. Their lives are severely limited by it.

Watching

Why do people stand around and watch when there is a fight at school? Why do some people fail to help when a person is attacked in the street? Human behaviour has not changed much over the years. In the Bible's story of the good Samaritan (Luke 10:25-37) the traveller was beaten up and left for dead. Two people ignored the victim. Why do you think they did this?

Vandals

Not all vandals are alike. There are the window-smashers, the paint-sprayers, the car-aerial-benders, the park-bench-carvers and the tyre-deflators – to name but a few. How would you answer each of these vandals?

I PAINT POLITICAL SLOGANS ON THE WALLS BECAUSE PEOPLE ROUND HERE NEED TO WAKE UP TO WHAT IS GOING ON!

IT'S BORING ROUND HERE! SMASHING THINGS UP GIVES YOU SOMETHING TO DO!

I broke his window because he reported me to the police for shoplifting.

I DO VANDALISM TO FRIGHTEN PEOPLE. I LIKE TO SEE THEIR STUPID FACES WHEN THEY'RE AFRAID.

I SMASH THINGS UP TO MAKE THEM NOTICE ME. THEY WON'T LISTEN TO REASON...

I ROB PHONE BOOTHS AND PARKING METERS COS I NEED THE CASH

Adults v children

Nearly two-thirds of all vandalism is carried out by adults. The only exception is objects placed on railway lines, which is largely carried out by children.

Looking after your image

Hooligans, thugs and vandals are very conscious of their hard image. Look at the poem on the next page. It shows that the image is often only a front. Why do you think some people need to see themselves as hard?

Unit 8

Subway graffiti in New York City. People have written graffiti on walls for thousands of years, but in this century, graffiti and vandalism have become closely linked.

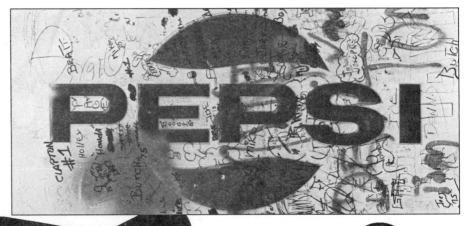

Nooligan

I'm a nooligan
don't give a toss
in our class
I'm the boss
(well, one of them)

I'm a nooligan
got a nard 'ead
step out of line
and you're dead
(well, bleedin)

I'm a nooligan
I spray me name
all over town
footballs me game
(well, watchin)

I'm a nooligan
violence is fun
gonna be a nassassin
or a hired gun
(well, a soldier)

Roger McGough

FOLLOW UP

1 Write a leaflet for the elderly which includes information on personal safety, home security suggestions, and advice to make them feel safer when out.

2 What are the consequences of vandalism? Look at this story. Peter and two of his friends lived near a motorway. One day, 'just for fun', as Peter put it, they dropped a brick from a footbridge onto a passing car. The brick fortunately went through the back window, harming no one, but the driver and passengers were very shaken and pulled in on the hard shoulder. A passer-by recognized the boys' school uniform and reported them to the police.
   What were the consequences of dropping the brick...

- on the people in the car?
- on the car itself?
- on the school?
- on Peter and his friends?
- on their parents?

3 Devise a short trial scene where a vandal is tried. The vandal must think up as many excuses or reasons for her or his vandalism as possible. What is the verdict of the class?

The angry brigade

In November 1605 Guy Fawkes and several other conspirators tried to blow up the government by placing explosives under the Houses of Parliament. A bomb planted in a Brighton Hotel in 1984, which was intended to blow up Mrs Thatcher and many members of her cabinet, echoed this early act of terrorism.

One group of British terrorists called themselves 'The Angry Brigade'. This is a name that could be applied to most groups of terrorists. Terrorism is brutal anger exercised on an international scale.

Spot the terrorist

One person's terrorist is another person's freedom fighter. When the Russian Red Army invaded Afghanistan in 1980, the Afghans were driven into the hills and began to fight back. The Russian soldiers regarded the rebels as terrorists, while many of the local people whose country had been taken over by Russia saw them as freedom fighters.

So what were they - terrorists or freedom fighters? Does it merely depend which side you are on, or has it something to do with motive and method?

Four case studies might help.

The French resistance

During World War II, the French resistance fought an underground campaign against the Germans who had invaded their country. They used bombs against German military targets, but innocent civilians were not deliberately bombed or maimed. The aim of the resistance was to overthrow the Nazis.

Nelson Mandela

Nelson Mandela is an African lawyer who has served a prison sentence of over twenty-five years. Mandela was part of the peaceful protests in South Africa prior to the 1960s and as a lawyer he fought for black rights. It was only after the Sharpeville massacre in 1960, when fifty-six black protestors were gunned down by

On the night of 12 October 1984, a powerful IRA bomb devastated Brighton's Grand Hotel. The Prime Minister and her cabinet narrowly escaped death.

police, that Mandela renounced the non-violent route to justice for black South Africans. He had exhausted all other avenues first. Many like Mandela were trapped between keeping a brutal and cruel law and the cause of truth and justice.

Nazir Hindawi
Nazir Hindawi took his pregnant Irish girlfriend to Heathrow Airport. She was booked on a flight to Israel. Unknown to her, Nazir had placed a bomb in her luggage to go off in mid-flight.

Nazir and his brother had grown up witnessing the plight of the Palestinians and were filled with hatred for the Jews. Fortunately, the bomb was discovered before she boarded the plane.

Ulricke Meinhof
Ulricke Meinhof came from an educated German background. She reacted against this and became part of the Baader-Meinhof group, whose bombing campaigns of the 1970s were carried on by the Red Army Faction.

Britain's most famous terrorist is Guy Fawkes, pictured with the other gunpowder plotters below. His arrest is celebrated every November 5th.

This group hated capitalism and hoped to bring about the downfall of western governments by inducing terror in the population by random bombing and kidnapping.

Which of the four groups would you say are terrorists?

Not all terrorists are the same
Terrorists act from different motives, even if they use similar tactics. There are many different types of terrorist. Some are motivated by religion, some fight for the rights of underprivileged groups, others fight for their national freedom, wanting their own state. Some groups such as the Red Brigade fight for political ideals - they want to change the way governments rule. What terrorists share are common methods.

Write a list of the methods terrorists use. Do you think any cause justifies the use of these?

Christian responses
On 13 May 1981, Pope John Paul II was shot as he was driven among the

Robert Winter — Christopher Wright — John Wright — Thomas Percy — Guido Fawkes — Robert Catesby — Thomas Win[...]

NCILIVM SEPT EM NOBILIVM ANGL ORVMCONIVRANTIVM IN NECEM IACOBI

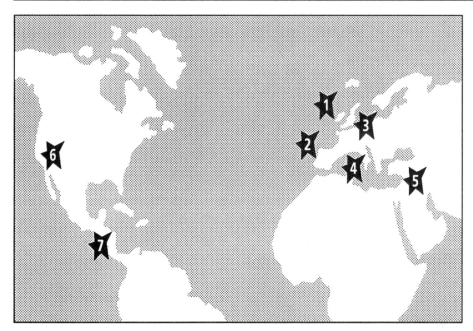

This map shows some of the locations of terrorist or freedom-fighter organizations that have been active since the early 1970s.
1 The IRA (Irish Republican Army).
2 ETA (the Basque separatists of northern Spain).
3 The Red Army Faction, formerly the Baader-Meinhof Gang, of West Germany.
4 The Red Brigades of Italy.
5 Various groups operate in the Middle East, including the PLO (Palestinian Liberation Organization) and Hezbollah.
6 The Symbionese Liberation Army in the United States.
7 The Contras of Nicaragua.

crowds of pilgrims in St Peter's Square, Rome. Mehmet Ali Agca, an Armenian terrorist, shot him to protest against the policies of the US and the USSR. The Pope was hit by four bullets and was raced to hospital. One eye-witness reported, 'It was awful. There was blood on the Pope's cassock.'

Two years later, Agca asked to see the Pope in his prison cell and begged his forgiveness, which the Pope gave. John Paul said, on emerging from the cell, 'What we told each other is a secret between us.'

The following are two other responses to terrorism...

Desmond Tutu, the Archbishop of Johannesburg, South Africa. He said that no change achieved by violence could escape being damaged and infected by it.
The Irish Catholic bishops. After the Enniskillen bomb blast in 1987, when many innocent people were killed, the bishops made it plain that for Catholics the choice was clear – good or evil. They maintained that nothing could justify the violence in Northern Ireland.

FOLLOW UP

1 Here are some suggestions made for combatting terrorism. What do you think of them? Can you add two suggestions of your own?
• a news blackout
• stricter airport controls
• international co-operation
• more highly-trained groups, such as the SAS

2 It has been said that people will listen to reasonable suggestions only if they feel that the only alternative is violence. Do you think this is true?

3 Make a police information sheet describing a terrorist, stating who they are, their background and what made them become a terrorist.

4 Find out one example of each of the following:
• A nationalist terrorist group
• A religious terrorist group
• A terrorist group which fights for the underprivileged

Anger and forgiveness

In this unit, we look at the story of Corrie Ten Boom. Corrie's story could have been a war story full of anger, hatred and bitterness, and no one would have blamed her. She was a survivor of the Nazi concentration camps. She had lost many members of her family and friends during the war. Although she had every right to be bitter and angry, her story is one of love and forgiveness.

Corrie Ten Boom, the Dutch watchmaker, whose story is a triumph of forgiveness over the evil of the Nazis.

The secret room

Corrie Ten Boom, a watchmaker's daughter, qualified as the first woman watchmaker in Holland. When Holland was occupied by the Nazis in 1940, Corrie, her sister Betsie and their father entered an unlikely new phase of their lives. The Ten Boom family had a secret room constructed in their home where they hid Jews from the Nazis.

Corrie and Betsie were middle-aged when they started this dangerous and exciting activity. They did not look like members of the underground, but that made them even more useful. Who would ever suspect two middle-aged spinsters?

For many months the hidden room sheltered Jews until the underground could arrange for their safe passage out of the country. But one day the Gestapo discovered it and Corrie, Betsie and their father were captured. Mr Ten Boom died shortly after his capture, but Corrie and Betsie were sent to Ravensbruck - one of the worst concentration camps.

Both Corrie and Betsie were Christians, and as they entered the hell of the camps they discovered that God was present even there. Many of the prisoners were filled with bitterness and hatred. But they saw hate give way to love, and unselfishness replace the selfishness that people resorted to in order to survive.

The back-breaking work affected Betsie's health and Corrie watched her sister become weaker and weaker. Despite her poor health, Betsie's main concern was for helping people after the war. She had a dream of opening a home for the victims of the camps. This dream was later to come true, although Betsie did not live to see it: she died in Ravensbruck.

After the war

Corrie survived the camps and lived to work among the mentally handicapped and camp victims. After a while she began to take in collaborators whom no one else would touch. Many people found it impossible to forgive their own countrymen who had betrayed them by aiding the enemy. The people Corrie cared for needed a lot of healing both in mind and body. They all needed to forgive someone: a sadistic guard, an informer, or maybe even themselves.

Corrie travelled widely, telling the story of Betsie and raising money for her work. One day when she was talking to a church congregation, something happened to make her realize that she was still bitter and had never forgiven the Germans for what they had done. A man came up to her, wanting to shake her hand. She remembered him as one of the guards who had sneered at her and Betsie as they were stripped and marched through the showers at Ravensbruck.

But the man had changed. He started to talk about how God had forgiven him and wiped out his past. Corrie realized that, although God had forgiven this man, she hadn't. Instead she was filled with anger and wanted to take revenge on him. She simply could not shake his hand. She realized that forgiving this man was impossible for her, so she prayed, 'Jesus I cannot forgive him. Give me your forgiveness.'

A sense of love overwhelmed her and she finally shook his hand. Although as a Christian Corrie had experienced God's forgiveness, she still needed God's help in order to forgive this man.

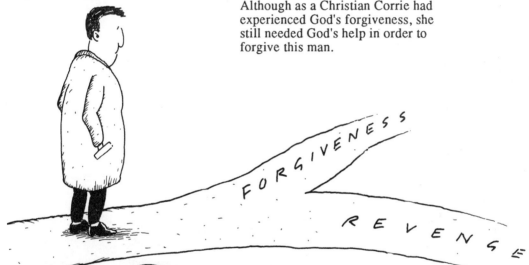

FOLLOW UP

1 What does it mean to forgive someone? Toni and her family were going away on holiday. They left Toni's pet dog with Tracy, one of Toni's best friends. When they arrived home after the holiday, Tracy's mum phoned to say that the dog had run off the week before, and was completely lost. Toni was angry and upset. In school the next day, Tracy avoided Toni. The day after that, Toni...

• walked up to Tracy and gave her a piece of her mind.
• swallowed her anger and spoke normally to Tracy without even mentioning the dog.
• ignored Tracy when she came up to speak to her.

Which of these is forgiveness? Give your reasons! If none of them is, then what do you think Toni could do if she wanted to forgive her friend?

2 Think back to a time recently when you either forgave someone or when someone forgave you. Write down what happened and how you felt. How did it affect your relationship with the other person?

You can read the rest of Corrie's story in *The Hiding Place*, published by Hodder and Stoughton.

Gandhi and the non-violent way

Gandhi refused to use violence or the methods of terrorism to gain India's independence. This still is taken from the film Gandhi.

When Mahatma Gandhi died he was mourned by people of many races and religions. He was a man who practised non-violence and yet was one of the most influential people in history. In this unit, we look at his life, and the way in which he won his battles without violence.

Gandhi's early life

Gandhi was born in 1869 to a reasonably well-off Hindu family. Gandhi was a shy and nervous child. He was frightened of the dark and was so scared of being teased that he used to run home from school as quickly as possible.

It was in England, where Gandhi came to study law, that some words of his own sacred text the Bhagavad-Gita deeply impressed him. 'The man who forsakes all desires and puts aside all pride of possession and pride in himself reaches the goal of supreme peace.' He was also affected by the teaching of Jesus, particularly the section in Matthew's Gospel (chapters 5-7) which is called the Sermon on the Mount.

In South Africa

Failing to find work as a lawyer in India, Gandhi moved to South Africa, where he had his first real taste of racial prejudice. One day while he was travelling on a train, he was told to move from his first-class seat to a third-class compartment, despite the fact that he had a first-class ticket. When he refused, he was thrown on the platform.

Gandhi thought over this incident and the widespread injustice which people suffered because of their race. As a result, he decided to stay in South Africa and fight for the rights of Indians living there.

Gandhi fought injustice in South Africa for twenty years. This struggle often landed him in prison, but his weapons were love exercised through non-violence. He believed that you couldn't fight wrong with force, and so he returned love for hate and respect for contempt – but he always held fast against injustice. Gandhi had names for his weapons: *satyagraha*, which means 'holding to the truth' and *ahimsa*, which means 'love through non-violence'.

The battle for India's independence
Gandhi returned to India in 1915 and he started to travel the country. Everywhere he went he met ignorance, poverty and ill-health. These were the first evils he wanted to fight. Then he wanted to fight the occupation of his country by the British. Gandhi wanted India to become independent, but he did not want this to happen by force. Nor did he want India to be torn by internal fighting between Muslims and Hindus. 'Before they think of freedom,' he said, 'they must be brave enough to love one another.'

Gandhi taught his followers that *satyagraha* (holding to the truth) is never the result of anger. It springs out of an inner conviction of truth. He also said that non-violence is not weakness. Instead it is a determination to love the enemy but never to give in. Gandhi successfully applied his teaching to many situations in India, organizing strikes and settling disputes.

On one occasion Gandhi's followers attempted the non-violent invasion of a

Non-violence

One of the religious texts which influenced Gandhi was:

You have heard that it was said, 'An eye for an eye and a tooth for a tooth.' But now I tell you: do not take revenge on someone who wrongs you. If anyone slaps you on the right cheek, let him slap your left cheek too. And if someone takes you to court to sue you for your shirt, let him have your coat as well. And if one of the occupation troops forces you to carry his pack one kilometre, carry it two kilometres. When someone asks you for something, give it to him; when someone wants to borrow something, lend it to him.

Jesus, speaking in Matthew 5:38-42.

government salt mine. Wave after wave of Gandhi's unarmed followers marched up to the 400 policemen who guarded the mine. They were badly beaten and some died. They also failed to take the mine. But their unequalled courage so impressed the world that people's thinking began to change.

When India finally gained its independence, the trouble was not over. As Gandhi had predicted, the Muslims and the Hindus fought each other in many bloody incidents. Gandhi refused to eat until the fighting in his area stopped and many joined him in his fast until peace was restored.

Gandhi's achievement

Gandhi died in 1948 as a victim of the violence he had taught against. Still weak from his fast, he was shot three times by a young man in the crowd outside his house. His assassin thought that his attempts to unite the Muslim and Hindu community were in some way responsible for atrocities committed against Hindus.

Gandhi, who had begun life as a shy, frightened little boy had grown into an internationally respected campaigner against injustice. He did not win all his battles. He failed to unite Muslims and Hindus, and India was eventually divided into Hindu India and Muslim Pakistan. Despite this, Gandhi did win many rights for his people and many solid victories. He was also a major force in achieving freedom for India, but he never once resorted to violence.

FOLLOW UP

1 What were the main problems faced by Gandhi in his fight for freedom?

2 What do you think of the words of Jesus (see the Non-violence box)? Do you think they are practical or impractical? How hard would you find it to put them into action?

3 Conduct an opinion poll of your class – or even of your year. Ask them what they think about the use of violence. Put this question to them:

When do you think it would be right to use violence?

- never, under any circumstances
- only on behalf of someone else
- only if my life was threatened
- only if I was under attack
- only if I thought someone was thinking of attacking me
- to show that I was really angry
- whenever I thought it would help me to get what I needed
- whenever I wanted

Work out from your poll how many people opted for each choice, and present your findings as a bar chart. What do you think of the results?

FOR SALE